FISHERY FARMING

How to Start, Run and Grow a Successful Fish Farm

MORRIS WILLIS

TABLE OF CONTENTS

INTRODUCTION

If you're looking for a profitable and fulfilling venture in agriculture, starting a fishery farm might just be the right fit for you. Fishery farming is the raising of domesticated fishes like chickens, ducks, and geese for meat, eggs, or feathers. Fishery products are highly sought after in the market, making fishery farming a lucrative business opportunity for small-scale farmers and entrepreneurs.

However, starting a fishery farm can be a daunting task, especially if you don't have prior knowledge of the industry. This book aims to provide you with a comprehensive guide on how to start and manage a successful fishery farm. Whether you're a beginner or a seasoned farmer, you'll find useful insights, practical tips, and expert advice in this book.

In this book, you'll learn the basics of the fishery industry, including its structure, market trends, and opportunities. You'll also discover how to identify your target customers and tailor your products to meet their needs. We'll guide you through the process of choosing the right fishery breed for your farm, taking into account factors such as climate, production goals, and market demand.

We'll also provide you with insights on how to build suitable housing and equipment for your fishes, ensuring their comfort and safety. You'll learn about feeding and nutrition requirements for optimal growth and health, as well as biosecurity measures to prevent disease outbreaks. We'll also cover egg and broiler production, hatchery management, and marketing and selling your fishery products.

Furthermore, we'll help you with financial planning for your fishery farm, including budgeting, investment, and risk management. You'll also learn about legal considerations and regulations, as well as managing your farm workforce. Additionally, we'll provide you with sustainable farming practices that promote environmental stewardship.

By the end of this book, you'll have a solid understanding of what it takes to start and manage a successful fishery farm. You'll also be equipped with the knowledge and skills necessary to scale up your fishery farm and tackle challenges that come with it. So let's get started on this exciting journey of raising chickens for profit!

Chapter 1:
Introduction to Fish Farming

Fish farming, known as aquaculture, has a rich history spanning thousands of years. It's a practice deeply embedded in human civilization's quest for sustenance, evolving from simple methods to sophisticated techniques employed today. This chapter delves into the evolution of aquaculture, underscores the significance of fish farming in addressing global food security challenges, and explores the diverse types of fish farming systems.

Aquaculture has quite a fascinating story that spans thousands of years. It's amazing how people have been figuring out ways to grow aquatic creatures for a really long time. Way back, civilizations like the Egyptians, Romans, and Chinese were already doing some pretty cool stuff with fish farming.

Around 4,000 years ago, the Chinese were like pioneers in fish farming. They started cultivating carp, which was a big deal and showed how they were onto something special with fish farming. And then, the Romans stepped in with their own take on it. They built these fancy fish ponds called piscinae, not just for food but also as a status symbol.

As time passed, different cultures added their own twists to fish farming. In Southeast Asia, they got creative by combining fish farming with growing rice. It was like a double win - better crops and fish at the same time!

Things got really interesting during the Industrial Revolution. That's when technology really started shaping modern fish farming. They figured out ways to hatch fish eggs artificially, which totally changed the game, allowing for mass production of fish. Fast forward to the 20th century, and boom - they introduced fish food and better ways to breed fish, making fish farming more efficient than ever.

Today, fish farming is a big deal. It's a key part of making sure we've got enough seafood to eat without putting too much strain on wild fish populations. And they're always coming up with new ways to make fish farming better, thinking about the environment and using cool new tech to make things work even smoother.

So, from ancient fish ponds to the high-tech fish farms we've got now, it's pretty awesome to see how people have been figuring out ways to feed us while taking care of the water and the fish at the same time.

Importance of Fish Farming in Global Food Security

Fish farming is a big deal when it comes to making sure we've got enough food worldwide. With more and more people to feed – we're talking about over 9 billion folks by 2050 – the need for food keeps going up. Fish are super nutritious, packing in essential proteins, vitamins, and those omega-3 fatty acids we all need for a healthy diet.

Why is fish farming so important for food security? Well, first off, it's a major source of protein, especially in places where other types of meat might not be as available. For folks struggling with not getting enough nutrients, fish can be a lifesaver.

Another huge reason is that it eases the pressure on wild fish populations. These days, fish in the wild are facing a tough time with overfishing and environmental changes. Fish farming helps take some of that load off by providing an alternative source of seafood while giving the wild fish a chance to bounce back.

But it's not just about food – fish farming is a big deal for local economies too. It creates jobs, especially in places near the water, giving folks a way to earn a living by producing and selling fish. And it's not just the farming itself; it also boosts other businesses related to making fish food, equipment, and getting fish from the farm to the market.

The cool thing about fish farming is how adaptable it is. It works in all sorts of places, from small ponds to huge commercial operations, which means it can fit into different areas and help out communities by providing food that's grown close by. That's pretty awesome since it cuts down on the need to transport food long distances, making it easier for everyone to get their hands on fresh fish.

So, fish farming isn't just about feeding people; it's about making sure everyone gets the right nutrients, taking some pressure off the oceans, boosting local economies, and finding sustainable ways to feed our growing population. It's like a superhero in the world of food security!

Types of Fish Farming Systems

Fish farming comes in different shapes and sizes, each tailored to suit various environments, fish species, and production goals. These systems offer diverse methods to raise fish sustainably and efficiently.

Pond Aquaculture
Pond aquaculture is one of the oldest and most traditional methods of fish farming. It involves using natural or artificially constructed ponds to rear fish. This system is adaptable and cost-effective, making it suitable for small-scale operations. Ponds provide a

controlled environment for fish, allowing farmers to manage water quality and feed the fish easily.

Cage Aquaculture
Cage aquaculture involves raising fish in cages or net enclosures submerged in natural water bodies like lakes, rivers, or coastal areas. These cages contain the fish while allowing water to flow freely through them. This system is often used for larger-scale operations and provides an environment where fish can grow in their natural habitat while being monitored and fed.

Recirculating Aquaculture Systems (RAS)
Recirculating Aquaculture Systems are closed-loop systems that recycle and filter water within a controlled environment. These systems minimize water usage by reusing it, making them highly efficient. RAS allows for intensive fish farming in indoor facilities, providing precise control over water quality parameters such as temperature and oxygen levels. It's commonly used for high-value fish species and in areas with limited access to natural water bodies.

Integrated Multi-Trophic Aquaculture (IMTA)
IMTA is an innovative approach that involves cultivating multiple species in a shared ecosystem. It aims to utilize waste produced by one species as nutrients for others, creating a symbiotic relationship between different organisms. For example, cultivating fish alongside seaweed or shellfish helps improve resource utilization and reduce environmental impact by utilizing the by-products of one species as food for another.

Aquaponics
Aquaponics is a system that combines aquaculture with hydroponics, where fish and plants are grown together in a mutually beneficial environment. Fish waste provides nutrients for

the plants, and the plants naturally filter the water, which is then recirculated back to the fish. It's an efficient and sustainable method that integrates fish and plant production, allowing for the simultaneous cultivation of both crops.

Each fish farming system has its advantages and considerations, offering a range of options for farmers to choose from based on their resources, goals, and environmental conditions. These systems continue to evolve, driving innovation and sustainability in the aquaculture industry.

The history of aquaculture showcases its adaptability and resilience, while its importance in global food security underscores the need for sustainable fish farming practices. Understanding the various fish farming systems lays the foundation for exploring the intricate world of aquaculture, setting the stage for the subsequent chapters' in-depth exploration.

Chapter 2:
Conducting a Market Analysis

Before starting a fish farm, it's essential to conduct a market analysis to identify potential customers and competitors in your target market. Understanding your target market, identifying consumer preferences, and assessing the competitive landscape are essential steps to make informed decisions and develop a profitable fishery farming business. This chapter outlines a comprehensive guide on conducting market research for your fish farm.

Market Research and Analysis

Diving into market research and analysis is like getting a roadmap to navigate the seas of the seafood industry. It's about digging deep into what's happening out there – understanding what people want, how they behave, and what's cooking in the market. First off, it's all about keeping your eyes peeled for what's trending. Are people raving about certain fish species? Is there a buzz around sustainably sourced seafood? Figuring out these trends helps predict where the market might be headed and how you can adjust your fish farming methods accordingly.

Then comes understanding what folks are craving and if you can match it. Get to know what fish products are hot in your target market. It's about figuring out what people like to eat based on where they live, their culture, and what they usually chow down on. At the same time, it's worth checking out what your competitors are up to – how they're doing things and where you might stand out.

Knowing what makes consumers tick is a big part of the game. It's all about understanding their taste buds, what they know about nutrition, and even how they like their fish packaged. This info is pure gold for shaping what you produce and how you sell it.

Plus, keeping an eye on the economic side of things and playing by the rules is crucial. Seeing how prices change, keeping tabs on costs, and making sure you're following all the regulations are part and parcel of the game.

Ultimately, doing a deep dive into market research and analysis in fish farming is like getting a compass for your business. It's about staying ahead of the curve, understanding what people want, and making your mark in the ever-changing world of fish farming. Being flexible and adapting to the market's waves is the name of the game.

Competitive Analysis

Once you've got a sense of what's happening in the market, it's time to turn your attention to the competition. Take a good look at the other players in the fish farming game – those farms around the corner or even the big fish farms across the globe – that are in the same league as yours, offering similar fish products.

What you want to do is really dig into what they're doing right and where they might be hitting a snag. Look at their strong points – maybe they're ace at marketing or have top-notch quality products. Equally important is understanding where they might be struggling – could be in pricing, distribution, or maybe even in keeping up with quality standards.

Pricing is a big one to suss out. Understanding how they price their products and what kind of market share they have can give you a good sense of how the fish farming market is operating.

Now, here's where the SWOT analysis really shines. It's like holding up a mirror to your own fish farming business. You get to see what you're awesome at – maybe it's your top-notch fish quality or excellent customer service. But it's equally important to spot areas that need a little work – maybe you're falling behind in marketing or need to streamline your production process.

Most importantly, doing this analysis helps spot those golden opportunities waiting to be grabbed or any threats looming on the horizon. It's all about seeing where your fish farming business fits in the big picture, understanding the lay of the land, and finding your own sweet spot in the market.

Consumer Behavior and Preferences

Getting into the minds of consumers is a game-changer in the fish farming world. It's all about understanding what gets them excited or turns them off when it comes to seafood. Ever wondered what flavors they prefer? Whether they're all about the nutritional benefits of fish? Or perhaps, if they're fussy about how the fish looks on the shelf? Knowing these details is key to tailoring your fish products and coming up with marketing strategies that really hit the mark.

The real insider's scoop comes from directly chatting with consumers. Surveys or feedback sessions are gold mines! It's like having a direct line to their thoughts, understanding what they like, what worries them, and what they're expecting when they pick up fish products. This kind of insight is pure gold – it helps tweak your products to fit what they're after and fine-tune your marketing strategies to really speak their language.

By figuring out their preferences, you're essentially crafting your fish products and marketing approaches in a way that ticks all the boxes for consumers. It's not just about selling fish; it's about creating products and messages that resonate with them, making sure they choose your fish over the others on the shelf.

Economic and Regulatory Factors

Economic factors are a big deal in the fish farming world. It's like watching the tide – keeping an eye on how prices are moving, what's up with fish product costs, and other economic signs that might sway how much folks are willing to shell out for fish.

Understanding these economic indicators helps fish farmers anticipate market shifts. Watching trends in pricing and production costs allows for making smart decisions about how to price their products competitively while maintaining profitability.

But that's not all; playing by the rules is non-negotiable. Knowing and sticking to the local and international regulations that oversee fish farming is crucial. These rules cover health and safety standards, environmental regulations, proper labeling, and obtaining necessary certifications to sell fish products.

Following these guidelines isn't just about following the law; it's also about building trust with consumers. It shows that your fish farming operation cares about their well-being, respects the environment, and is committed to delivering safe and high-quality fish products. Ultimately, this adherence to regulations isn't just about compliance; it's about maintaining integrity and ensuring a sustainable future for fish farming.

A solid market analysis is like a compass guiding your fish farming ship. By understanding the market trends, what consumers want, who your competition is, and playing by the rules, you're better equipped to craft savvy marketing plans, tweak products to match consumer needs, and stand out in the fish farming world. Staying updated with market changes keeps your business nimble and successful in the ever-evolving world of fish farming.

Chapter 3:
Creating a Business Plan

A well-structured business plan is the cornerstone of a successful fish farming venture. It serves as a roadmap, guiding your decisions, setting clear goals, and ensuring efficient resource allocation. This guide outlines the essential components of a business plan for your fishery farm, helping you build a solid foundation for your business's growth and prosperity.

Executive Summary:
Begin with an executive summary that provides a concise overview of your fishery farm business. Highlight the mission, vision, and goals of your farm, along with a summary of your key strategies for success. This section should capture the essence of your entire plan and entice readers to delve further.

Business Description:
Detail the nature of your fishery farm, explaining whether it's focused on fingerlings production, fish production, or both. Describe your target market, the competitive landscape, and the unique value proposition that sets your farm apart from others.

Market Analysis:
Conduct a thorough market analysis to understand the demand for fishery products in your region. Identify your target customers, their preferences, and purchasing behavior. Analyze competitors' strengths and weaknesses, and outline how you plan to position your farm to capitalize on market opportunities.

Products and Services:
Outline the specific fishery products you intend to offer. Describe the breeds you'll raise, the quality standards you'll maintain, and any specialty products you might consider, such as organic or free-

range fishery. Highlight the benefits your products bring to customers.

Operations and Management:
Detail the day-to-day operations of your fishery farm. Describe the facilities, equipment, and processes you'll use for feeding, housing, disease control, and waste management. Also, introduce the key members of your management team, highlighting their relevant expertise and roles.

Marketing and Sales Strategy:
Explain your approach to marketing and selling your fishery products. Outline your promotional activities, distribution channels, pricing strategy, and methods for building brand awareness and customer loyalty.

Financial Projections:
Present detailed financial projections for your fishery farm. Include income statements, balance sheets, and cash flow statements for the first few years of operation. Consider factors such as initial investment, operating expenses, revenue forecasts, and profitability milestones.

Funding and Investment:
If seeking external funding, outline your funding requirements and how you plan to secure the necessary capital. This could include personal savings, loans, grants, or investor contributions. Provide a breakdown of how the funds will be allocated and repaid.

Risk Assessment and Mitigation:
Identify potential risks and challenges that your fishery farm might face, such as disease outbreaks, market fluctuations, or regulatory changes. Discuss strategies to mitigate these risks, showcasing your preparedness and adaptability.

Implementation Timeline:
Create a timeline that outlines the key milestones and activities required to launch and grow your fishery farm. This timeline will serve as a practical guide for tracking your progress and ensuring that you stay on course.

Exit Strategy:
Although often overlooked, having a clear exit strategy is crucial. Describe your plans in case you decide to sell or transition your fishery farm in the future. This could involve selling to a successor, merging with another farm, or other options.

Crafting a thorough business plan for your fishery farm is a foundational step that contributes to the long-term success of your venture. A well-structured plan not only helps you make informed decisions but also demonstrates your commitment and professionalism to potential investors, lenders, and partners. By addressing each section meticulously, you'll create a roadmap that charts the course to realizing your fishery farming aspirations.

Chapter 4:
Securing Funding for Your Fish Farm

Starting a fishery farm requires a significant amount of capital, which can be a challenge for many new entrepreneurs. Securing funding for your fishery farm is a crucial step in getting your business off the ground. In this chapter, we'll explore some of the funding options available to fishery farmers.

Personal Savings:
Utilizing your personal savings is one of the most straightforward ways to fund your fishery farm. It demonstrates your commitment and dedication to your venture. Carefully assess your financial situation and determine how much of your savings you can allocate without jeopardizing your personal financial stability.

Traditional Loans:
Bank loans are a common avenue for securing funds. Approach local banks or credit unions to inquire about business loans tailored to agriculture or small businesses. Prepare a solid business plan that outlines your fishery farm's potential profitability, which will be crucial in convincing lenders of your repayment capacity.

Government Grants and Subsidies:
Government agencies often provide grants, subsidies, and incentives to support agricultural ventures, including fishery farming. Research and identify relevant programs at the federal, state, or local levels. These funds can significantly reduce your initial investment burden.

Investors and Partnerships:
Consider seeking investors or forming partnerships with individuals or organizations interested in the agriculture sector. Investors may provide funds in exchange for equity or a share of profits.

Partnerships can bring not only financial support but also valuable expertise and networks.

Crowdfunding and Online Platforms:
Crowdfunding platforms and online fundraising campaigns can help you access a broader network of potential supporters. Create compelling campaigns that highlight your fishery farm's mission, value proposition, and potential impact. Platforms like Kickstarter, Indiegogo, or specialized agricultural crowdfunding platforms can be explored.

Venture Capital and Angel Investors:
Venture capital firms and angel investors who specialize in agriculture or food-related industries might be interested in supporting innovative fishery farm projects. Craft a strong pitch that highlights the unique aspects of your farm and its growth potential to attract these investors.

Agricultural Co-operatives:
Joining or forming agricultural co-operatives can provide access to pooled resources and shared funding opportunities. Co-operatives often collaborate to secure bulk purchases, access loans, and market products collectively, providing financial advantages.

Microloans and Microfinance:
Microfinance institutions offer smaller loans tailored to micro-entrepreneurs and small-scale businesses. These loans can be particularly suitable for individuals looking to start small or expand incrementally. Research microfinance institutions in your region.

Supplier Financing and Barter:
Negotiate with suppliers for deferred payment terms or trade agreements. Some suppliers may be willing to provide financing for equipment or inputs in exchange for future business. This can ease your initial financial burden.

Selling Shares:
If your fishery farm is structured as a corporation or partnership, you could raise funds by selling shares to investors. This strategy allows you to gather capital while spreading the financial risk among shareholders.

Securing funds for your fishery farm requires careful planning, research, and a strategic approach. Evaluate the options available based on your financial situation, business plan, and long-term goals. Combining multiple funding sources, such as personal savings, loans, grants, and partnerships, can provide a balanced and diversified approach to funding your fishery farm's growth. Remember that each funding option comes with its own terms and considerations, so it's essential to thoroughly assess the benefits and potential risks before making a decision.

Chapter 5:
Finding and Purchasing Land for Your Fish Farm

Finding and purchasing land for your fishery farm is a significant step in starting your business that demands meticulous attention to a range of crucial factors. The location of the land is of paramount importance, with accessibility being a key consideration. Optimal placement near major roads and transportation networks not only ensures smooth logistical operations for the movement of feed, fishery, and products but also facilitates efficient connectivity to urban centers or markets, thereby enhancing distribution and sales prospects. As you embark on this journey, it's imperative to delve into local zoning regulations and land-use ordinances to ascertain that the chosen land is in alignment with agricultural or fishery farming activities. Complying with these regulations isn't just a matter of adherence; it's a safeguard against potential legal complications and a means to secure essential permits that propel your farm forward.

The quality of the soil and its drainage characteristics are paramount aspects in assessing land suitability. Thoroughly evaluating soil composition, fertility, and drainage capacity can significantly impact the health of your shoal and, if you're considering cultivating feed crops, the overall agricultural productivity. The topography and elevation of the land also merit careful evaluation. Opting for land with flat or gently sloping terrain streamlines construction and facilitates effective drainage, whereas steep slopes can give rise to challenges like runoff and erosion that could hinder optimal fishery farm operations.

In your search, the surrounding environmental factors assume pivotal roles. Conduct a comprehensive analysis of the land's proximity to bodies of water, industrial sites, and residential areas. It's prudent to steer clear of regions susceptible to flooding, as excessive water accumulation can disrupt your fishery operations and pose potential health hazards to the fishes. Moreover, the availability of essential infrastructure and utilities should not be underestimated. Access to reliable electricity, water supply, and communication networks are essential components in upholding the efficiency and functionality of your fishery farm.

In tandem with these considerations, ponder over the land's size in relation to your fishery farm's intended scale of production and future expansion aspirations. Foresight is key; considering the potential for future growth and diversification allows you to invest in a land parcel that will accommodate your evolving needs. Biosecurity, a paramount concern in fishery farming, necessitates that you opt for a location that mitigates the risk of disease transmission. To this end, steer clear of areas characterized by high fishery density or proximity to other livestock operations, thereby fortifying the health and wellness of your shoal.

Additionally, it's wise to scrutinize neighboring farms and their agricultural practices. Ideally, neighboring farms should engage in compatible activities to reduce the likelihood of cross-contamination and other associated challenges. Naturally, cost is a determining factor, so evaluating your budget for land acquisition is fundamental. It's not solely the purchase price that matters; you must also factor in ancillary expenses such as land preparation, infrastructure development, and adherence to regulatory prerequisites.

In summation, the process of identifying the perfect land for your fishery farm necessitates a holistic and exhaustive approach. With meticulous consideration of factors ranging from location and accessibility to environmental conditions, biosecurity, and financial feasibility, you can make an educated and calculated decision that lays the foundation for a thriving and sustainable fishery farming venture.

Purchasing the Land

Once you've found the right piece of land, the next step is to purchase it. Acquiring the perfect piece of land for your envisioned fishery farm embarks upon a transformative journey from concept to tangible reality, where each step taken is akin to laying a crucial building block of your agricultural dream. The process of purchasing land is multifaceted, necessitating meticulous planning, prudent due diligence, and unwavering attention to legal and financial intricacies. Within this journey lies a sequence of critical steps, each contributing to the creation of a harmonious and successful fishery farming venture.

The initial stride involves the determination of your budget, a foundational pillar that outlines the financial scope of your land acquisition endeavor. It's not just the direct cost of the land that should be considered; ancillary expenses such as legal fees, land surveys, environmental assessments, and the potential development of infrastructure must be encompassed within this financial framework. This budget serves as a compass, guiding your decisions throughout the process.

With budget in hand, the exploration of suitable properties unfolds. This entails a meticulous search through a myriad of real estate listings, collaborating with experts specializing in agricultural properties, and delving into local classifieds. The objective is to unearth lands that harmonize with the distinct requisites of your fishery farm, taking into account factors like location, size, zoning regulations, soil quality, topography, and the proximity to vital services that ensure seamless operations.

However, a superficial overview won't suffice; a thorough inspection of potential lands is imperative. Engage in site visits to experience the land firsthand. Evaluate soil quality, drainage patterns, potential environmental concerns, and adherence to zoning regulations. Collaborating with professionals like land surveyors and environmental experts amplifies the depth and accuracy of these assessments, providing a comprehensive understanding of the land's suitability.

No land acquisition process is complete without legal consultation. Seasoned attorneys proficient in real estate transactions and agricultural regulations serve as invaluable guides, navigating you through intricate legal complexities. They meticulously scrutinize property deeds, titles, and any existing encumbrances to ensure a seamless and legitimate transfer of ownership. They also assist in the intricate negotiation process and the drafting of contracts that safeguard your interests.

Navigating negotiations skillfully, you proceed to the crucial stage of offer submission. Crafting a well-structured written offer encapsulating the terms and conditions of the purchase, including purchase price, down payment, contingencies, and projected closing date, marks this step. As you advance, aligning your financing requirements with a mortgage application becomes essential. Banks and financial institutions assess your business plan, financial statements, and credit history before granting approval and outlining loan terms.

The synthesis of these steps culminates in the creation of a comprehensive purchase agreement, carefully curated in collaboration with your attorney. This legally binding document encapsulates the transaction's core terms and conditions. After a meticulous review, your signature seals this agreement, setting the stage for the subsequent contingency period. During this phase, any stipulated conditions, such as soil tests or environmental assessments, are meticulously fulfilled.

As the deal's closure approaches, the finality of the transaction looms. Your attorney and the seller's representative orchestrate this transition, ensuring seamless ownership transfer, financial settlement, and the endorsement of legal documentation. Once this is accomplished, the baton of ownership is officially passed to you, signifying your possession of the property and unlocking the potential for the development of your fishery farm operations.

In essence, the process of purchasing land for your fishery farm embodies a meticulous and dynamic journey. With each step carefully choreographed, from budgeting and property evaluation to legal consultation, negotiation, and documented agreements, you craft a solid and sustainable foundation for your burgeoning fishery farm enterprise. Through unwavering commitment to due diligence and a systematic approach, you not only acquire land but also set the stage for the realization of your fishery farming aspirations.

Finding and purchasing land for your fishery farm is a significant step in starting your business. It's important to consider factors such as location, zoning and regulations, land quality, and cost when selecting land for your fishery farm. Once you've found the right piece of land, it's important to work with a qualified real estate attorney to ensure that the purchase process goes smoothly. In the next chapter, we'll explore the process of designing and building your fishery farm.

Chapter 6:
Planning Your Fish Farm

Planning is key when it comes to setting up a fish farm. This chapter dives into the important steps involved in planning: picking the right fish, finding the best location, and understanding the legal aspects of fish farming.

Choosing the Right Fish Species

Picking the fish species for your farming venture is a big call. There's a whole array of options out there, each with its unique requirements and perks:

Tilapia: These fish are like the superheroes of fish farming. They're tough cookies, growing real quick, and can handle a variety of water conditions. People love them for their mild taste and high protein content, making them a hit in many markets.

Catfish: Picture these fellas as the all-rounders. They're hardy, flavorful, and adaptable. Whether it's ponds or Recirculating Aquaculture Systems (RAS), they thrive. Catfish have firm flesh, making them a sought-after choice in many places.

Salmon: Ah, the kings of flavor and nutrition. But, they're a bit finicky. Salmon need their water cold and packed with oxygen, so they usually hang out in cages in freshwater or the big blue. Their distinct taste and nutrients make them quite the catch for consumers.

Trout: These buddies are pretty much like salmon's cousins. They share the love for chilly, well-oxygenated water. You'll find them chilling in ponds, raceways, or even in cage systems.

When it comes to picking the right species, it's all about weighing their needs against what you can offer. Consider factors like the market demand for each type, their compatibility with your farming method, and how well you can meet their specific needs. Finding that sweet spot where the fish species align with your farming style and have good market potential is key to reeling in success.

Picking the Perfect Location

Choosing the right location for your fish farm is a crucial decision. Here's what to consider:

Climate: Each fish species has its climate sweet spot. Understanding your local climate helps match the fish to the weather. Whether it's warm, cool, or somewhere in between, finding the right temperature range for your chosen fish species is key. For instance, some fish thrive in warmer waters, while others prefer cooler temperatures. Understanding whether your area offers the right conditions for warmth, coolness, or a bit of both throughout the year helps in picking the fish and planning their growth cycle. Here are the general temperature ranges preferred by some common fish species often found in aquaculture:

Tilapia: They thrive in temperatures between 77°F to 86°F (25°C to 30°C). These fish can tolerate a wide range of temperatures, but they grow best in warm water.

Catfish: They prefer temperatures around 75°F to 80°F (24°C to 27°C). Catfish can tolerate varying temperatures, but their growth is optimal within this range.

Salmon: These fish like colder waters, usually between 50°F to 60°F (10°C to 15°C). Their ideal temperature range contributes to their flavor and growth.

Trout: Similar to salmon, trout also prefer colder temperatures, ranging from 50°F to 60°F (10°C to 15°C). They thrive in well-oxygenated, cool water environments.

These temperature ranges serve as guidelines for optimal growth and health of these fish species. However, it's essential to consider other environmental factors alongside temperature to ensure the overall well-being of the fish in aquaculture settings. Factors such as water quality, oxygen levels, and suitable habitat conditions play crucial roles in fish health and growth.

Water Quality: Fish are pretty picky about their water quality. Testing factors like pH levels, oxygen content, and cleanliness is essential. Maintaining optimal water quality ensures a healthy habitat for your fish. Regular checks and adjustments keep the water conditions just right for your aquatic friends.

Land and Accessibility: Finding the ideal piece of land is like finding treasure. You'll need space for ponds and easy access to water sources. Additionally, being close to markets or transport links is advantageous. Having land suitable for constructing ponds and being conveniently located for transportation eases the logistics of getting your fish to market.

Ultimately, the perfect location offers the optimal climate conditions for your fish species, ensures excellent water quality, and provides the accessibility you need for a successful fish farming operation. Matching your fish's needs with the right environmental conditions sets the stage for a thriving farm.

Understanding Laws and Regulations

Running a fish farm involves navigating through a web of regulations and permits. Here's what to keep in mind:

Permits: Before diving into fish farming waters, it's crucial to secure the necessary permissions. This could involve obtaining environmental permits and aquaculture licenses from relevant authorities. These permits give you the green light to set up and operate your fish farm legally.

Environmental Regulations: Staying on the right side of environmental rules is a must. Adhering to standards related to waste management, responsible water usage, and safeguarding natural habitats is critical. These regulations ensure that your fish farming practices don't harm the environment and contribute to maintaining ecological balance.

Safety and Hygiene: Ensuring the safety and health of both your fish and consumers is paramount. Abiding by food safety regulations and maintaining impeccable hygiene standards in your farming operation is essential. This ensures that the fish produced meet quality standards and are safe for consumption. It's not just about regulations; it's about everyone's well-being.

Understanding and complying with these rules and regulations isn't just about ticking boxes; it's about operating responsibly. It helps steer clear of legal issues, minimizes environmental impact, ensures the health and safety of your fish, and maintains a positive reputation for your fish farm. Ultimately, responsible operation ensures sustainable and ethical fish farming practices.In short, taking the time to plan things out properly—choosing the right fish, finding a good spot, and understanding the rules—lays a strong foundation for a successful fish farming venture.

Chapter 7:
Setting Up Your Fish Farm

Once you've planned the basics, it's time to put things into action and set up your fish farm. This chapter focuses on the practical aspects: building the structures for your fish, managing the water they live in, and using the right equipment and technology to ensure their well-being.

Designing and Constructing Ponds, Tanks, or Cages

Designing and constructing the right environment for your fish farm is crucial for their well-being and growth. Depending on your fish species and resources, you'll choose between ponds, tanks, or cages.

Ponds: Building ponds involves shaping the land to create suitable water bodies for fish. These can be natural or man-made and are versatile, catering to various species and farm sizes. Ponds provide a more natural setting for fish, allowing them space to swim and grow.

Tanks: Tanks offer a controlled environment for fish farming. Available in different sizes and materials like concrete, fiberglass, or plastic, tanks are versatile and commonly used in Recirculating Aquaculture Systems (RAS) for intensive fish farming. They provide precise control over water quality and environmental conditions.

Cages: These structures are placed in natural water bodies such as rivers, lakes, or oceans to contain and grow fish. Cages allow farming in open water while managing the fish's environment. They offer an efficient way to utilize natural water resources for farming.

Each structure has its perks and requires specific planning and construction for optimal fish growth and health. Factors like the fish species, available space, water resources, and farming goals influence the choice of structure. Designing and constructing these environments tailored to your fish's needs ensure a conducive and thriving habitat for successful fish farming.

Water Management: Oxygenation, Filtration, and Monitoring

Ensuring top-notch water quality is a fish farming priority. Here's what's involved in maintaining that aqua-perfection:

Oxygenation: Think of oxygen as the lifeblood of your fish farm. Making sure there's enough oxygen in the water is a big deal. Aeration systems like diffusers or aerators come to the rescue, especially in crowded fish areas or when the weather's warm and oxygen levels tend to dip. These systems keep the water oxygen-rich, ensuring your fish are breathing easy.

Filtration: Just like cleaning your fishbowl, filtration systems here do the job of tidying up the water. They sift out waste and gunk, keeping the water sparkling clean. There are different types of filters – mechanical, biological, or a combo of both – depending on your setup. These filters work tirelessly to keep the water in top-notch condition for your fish pals.

Monitoring: Keeping an eye on water quality is like being a fish detective. Regularly checking parameters like temperature, pH levels, dissolved oxygen, and ammonia is crucial. Monitoring devices and nifty test kits help keep tabs on these parameters, ensuring everything stays just right for your fishy friends.

Maintaining that pristine water quality isn't just about keeping things pretty. It's the key to keeping your fish healthy and disease-free. By managing water quality effectively, you're setting the stage for your fish to thrive and ensuring their overall well-being. After all, happy fish mean a happy fish farmer!

Equipment and Technology: Aeration Systems, Feeders, and Monitoring Devices

Using the right equipment and technology can streamline operations and improve efficiency:

Aeration Systems: A fish farmer's best friend, aeration systems, ensure there's enough oxygen in the water for your fish to breathe easy. These systems come in various forms, such as diffusers or aerators, and they work their magic, especially in densely stocked areas or during warm weather when oxygen levels might drop. By oxygenating the water, these systems maintain a healthy aquatic environment for your fish.

Feeders: Think of feeders as the mealtime organizers for your fish. Automatic feeders or feeding systems ensure your fish get their meals at the right time and in the right quantities. These handy devices not only save time but also ensure that your fish receive the necessary nutrition to grow healthily.

Monitoring Devices: Keeping an eye on the aquatic world is where monitoring devices shine. These gadgets track essential parameters like water temperature, pH levels, dissolved oxygen, and ammonia concentrations. Whether it's simple test kits or high-tech monitoring devices, these tools help fish farmers stay informed about their fish's environment, ensuring optimal conditions for growth and health.

Having the right equipment and technology on your fish farm is like having a reliable team to support you. Aeration systems keep the oxygen flowing, feeders ensure your fish never miss a meal, and monitoring devices help you stay on top of water quality. Together, they play a crucial role in maintaining a healthy and thriving environment for your fish, contributing to a successful fish farming operation.

In essence, setting up your fish farm involves creating the right environment, managing water quality, and using appropriate equipment and technology to ensure the well-being and successful growth of your fish.

Chapter 8:
Fish Health and Nutrition

Ensuring the well-being and proper nutrition of your fish is crucial for a successful fish farming operation. This chapter delves into understanding fish health, feeding strategies, and sustainable nutrition practices.

Understanding Fish Health

Keeping your fish in top-notch health requires a proactive approach to prevent diseases and effective strategies to manage any issues that arise:

Prevention: As the old saying goes, prevention is better than cure. Maintaining optimal water quality, providing proper nutrition, and conducting regular health checks for your fish can significantly reduce the risk of diseases. Implementing quarantine procedures for new fish arrivals helps prevent the introduction of potential pathogens to your established population.

Management: Despite all preventive measures, fish can still fall ill. Quick identification of diseases and taking appropriate actions, which might involve administering medication or adjusting environmental conditions, are crucial steps to contain and minimize the impact of diseases. Timely and accurate responses can prevent diseases from spreading throughout the fish population.

Regular observation is the key; keeping a keen eye on your fish helps detect any signs of illness early on. This allows for swift action to be taken, potentially preventing a minor issue from becoming a major health problem for your fish. Collaborating with aquatic veterinarians or experts is also invaluable. Their expertise can provide guidance on disease management, treatment protocols, and best practices to ensure the health and well-being of your fish.

Common Diseases in Fishes

In fish farming, several common diseases can affect fish health. Here are a few along with their symptoms and treatments:

1. Ichthyophthirius multifiliis (Ich):
Symptoms: Ich, also known as white spot disease, appears as white spots resembling grains of salt on the fish's body, fins, and gills. Infected fish may show signs of irritation, rubbing against objects, and reduced appetite.

Treatment: Ich can be treated with medications containing formalin or malachite green. Raising water temperature slightly can also help as it accelerates the lifecycle of the parasite, making it more susceptible to medication.

2. Columnaris Disease:
Symptoms: Columnaris causes lesions on the skin, gills, and fins, appearing as white or grayish patches. Infected fish may exhibit lethargy, loss of appetite, and redness around the affected areas.

Treatment: Antibiotics like oxytetracycline or potassium permanganate baths are commonly used for treatment. Improving water quality and reducing stressors can also aid in recovery.

3. Aeromoniasis:
Symptoms: Aeromoniasis manifests as red sores, ulcers, or lesions on the fish's skin or fins. Affected fish may display abnormal swimming patterns, lack of appetite, and inflammation at the site of the sores.

Treatment: Antibiotics like florfenicol or sulfonamides are effective in treating Aeromoniasis. Maintaining good water quality and reducing overcrowding can prevent its spread.

4. Dropsy:
Symptoms: Dropsy causes bloating, swelling of the abdomen, protruding scales, and raised scales resembling a pinecone. Infected fish may also exhibit buoyancy issues and lethargy.

Treatment: There's no specific medication for Dropsy, but improving water quality, maintaining low-stress environments, and using antibacterial treatments can help manage symptoms.

5. Fungal Infections:
Symptoms: Fungal infections appear as white cotton-like growths on the skin, fins, or gills. Infected fish might show signs of irritation, reduced activity, and loss of appetite.

Treatment: Antifungal medications like formalin or salt baths are commonly used for treating fungal infections. Addressing underlying causes such as poor water quality can prevent their occurrence.

Prompt identification of symptoms and timely treatment are crucial in managing diseases in fish farming. However, prevention through good husbandry practices, maintaining optimal water quality, providing proper nutrition, and reducing stressors remains the best approach to minimize the risk of diseases in fish farms. Seeking advice from aquatic veterinarians or experts can further assist in disease management and prevention strategies.

By combining proactive preventive measures with swift and appropriate management strategies, fish farmers can maintain good fish health and minimize the impact of diseases on their aquatic livestock. Early detection, prompt action, and seeking expert advice are fundamental elements in effectively managing fish health on a fish farm.

Feeding Strategies and Nutrition Requirements for Different Fish Species

Feeding strategies and nutrition requirements vary among different fish species in aquaculture. Understanding these variations is key to ensuring optimal growth and health for the fish. Here are some general guidelines for different fish species:

1. Tilapia:
Feeding Strategy: Tilapia are omnivorous and have a flexible diet. They readily consume plant-based feeds but also thrive on animal-based protein sources.

Nutrition Requirements: They require a balanced diet with proteins, carbohydrates, fats, vitamins, and minerals. Commercial pellets or formulated feeds often meet their nutritional needs.

2. Catfish:
Feeding Strategy: Catfish are omnivorous bottom-feeders and primarily feed on plant matter, insects, and small fish.

Nutrition Requirements: Their diet includes proteins, fats, and carbohydrates. Commercial feeds formulated with appropriate protein content often suffice for catfish nutrition.

3. Salmon:
Feeding Strategy: Salmon are carnivorous and primarily consume fish meal or fish oil-based feeds.

Nutrition Requirements: They require high-protein diets rich in essential amino acids and omega-3 fatty acids for growth. Feeds designed specifically for salmon often contain fish meal and other marine ingredients to meet their nutritional needs.

4. Trout:
Feeding Strategy: Trout are carnivorous and prefer high-protein diets, consuming a variety of small aquatic animals.

Nutrition Requirements: They require feeds rich in proteins, amino acids, and fats for optimal growth. Pelleted feeds formulated with fish meal or other protein sources are commonly used.

5. Carp:
Feeding Strategy: Carp are omnivorous and can consume a wide range of natural food sources, including plants, insects, and small fish.

Nutrition Requirements: They benefit from diets containing both plant-based and animal-based proteins, along with carbohydrates. Formulated feeds tailored for carp provide a balanced diet.

Understanding the feeding behavior and nutritional requirements specific to each fish species is crucial in developing appropriate feeding strategies. Commercially available feeds formulated to meet the nutritional needs of these species are commonly used in aquaculture practices. Adjusting feeding regimes, portion sizes, and feed compositions according to the specific needs of each species supports their growth, health, and overall well-being in fish farming operations.

Sustainable and Environmentally Friendly Feed Options

Research and Innovation: Continuous research and innovation in feed technology are essential for developing feeds that not only support fish health and growth but also prioritize environmental sustainability. Advancements in feed formulation that minimize environmental impact, enhance nutrient absorption, and reduce reliance on unsustainable resources are key to sustainable aquaculture practices.

Embracing sustainable feed options isn't just an environmental win; it's a crucial step toward ensuring the long-term viability and success of fish farming. By adopting practices that prioritize sustainability in feed production, fish farmers contribute to the preservation of aquatic ecosystems and pave the way for a more sustainable future for aquaculture.

In essence, prioritizing fish health through preventive measures and effective management, understanding and meeting their nutritional requirements, and embracing sustainable feed options are essential aspects of responsible fish farming.

Chapter 9:
Managing the Fish Farm Operation

Running a fish farm smoothly requires careful attention to daily tasks, growth monitoring, and ensuring a healthy environment for the fish. This chapter focuses on the practical aspects of managing the farm on a day-to-day basis.

Daily Operations and Maintenance

In fish farming, daily operations and maintenance are crucial aspects ensuring the farm runs smoothly. Daily tasks encompass a range of activities, from monitoring water quality parameters to feeding the fish. Regular checks on water temperature, pH levels, dissolved oxygen, and ammonia content are imperative to maintain optimal conditions for the fish. Additionally, feeding schedules need to be adhered to, ensuring the fish receive the required nutrition for their growth and health. Observing the fish behavior and overall health is part of the routine, allowing for early detection of any signs of illness or stress.

Apart from fish care, daily operations involve maintaining the infrastructure of the farm. This includes checking and maintaining equipment such as aeration systems, filters, tanks, or cages to ensure they function efficiently. Cleaning and regular upkeep of ponds, tanks, or cage systems are necessary to prevent the accumulation of waste and debris that could affect water quality.

Moreover, record-keeping forms an integral part of daily operations. Keeping detailed records of water quality parameters, feeding schedules, fish health observations, and any maintenance performed helps track the farm's performance and assists in making informed decisions for future operations. The meticulous attention to these daily tasks ensures the overall well-being of the fish, optimal farm productivity, and the sustainability of the fish farming operation.

Stocking Density and Growth Monitoring

Stocking density and growth monitoring are pivotal in running a fish farm smoothly. Stocking density refers to how many fish share a specific space or volume of water in the farm. It's like finding the sweet spot — too many fish crowded together can lead to competition for food and space, stressing them out. But if there are too few fish, it might not make the best use of the farm resources.

Keeping an eye on the growth of the fish is just as important. This means regularly checking how big they're getting, how much they weigh, and how they're developing. Monitoring growth helps us understand if the fish are doing well and if our feeding methods and farm conditions are working effectively. It's like a health check-up for the fish, guiding us on how to adjust feeding routines or manage the environment for their best growth.

Getting the balance right between stocking density and keeping a close watch on fish growth is the secret sauce to a successful fish farm. It's about making sure the fish have enough room to thrive and using that information to ensure they're growing healthy and strong.

Water Quality Management and Environmental Sustainability

Water quality management is the cornerstone of environmental sustainability in fish farming. Maintaining optimal water conditions is crucial not just for the health and well-being of the fish but also for the surrounding environment. Effective water quality management involves monitoring various parameters such as pH levels, dissolved oxygen content, ammonia levels, temperature, and more.

Ensuring these parameters remain within acceptable ranges is vital to prevent adverse effects on fish health and the ecosystem. High ammonia levels or low oxygen content, For instance, ideal pH levels typically range between 6.5 to 8.5, ensuring a suitable environment for fish health. Dissolved oxygen should be maintained at 5 milligrams per liter or higher to support fish respiration. Additionally, keeping ammonia levels below 0.02 milligrams per liter helps prevent stress in fish. Monitoring temperature within the range suitable for the specific fish species being farmed is crucial. These parameters ensure a healthy aquatic environment for the fish while also minimizing negative impacts on the surrounding ecosystem. Striving to maintain these acceptable parameters is key to sustaining a healthy and environmentally friendly fish farming operation.

Moreover, poor water quality can negatively impact the surrounding environment if not managed properly, leading to issues such as algal blooms or contamination of natural water bodies.

Adopting sustainable practices in water management is key to environmental stewardship in fish farming. Implementing technologies like recirculating aquaculture systems (RAS) that efficiently filter and maintain water quality or employing natural and biological filtration methods are steps toward sustainability. Additionally, reducing nutrient runoff and waste disposal into surrounding water bodies helps mitigate environmental impact.

Ultimately, effective water quality management not only ensures the health of the fish but also plays a pivotal role in maintaining a sustainable and environmentally friendly fish farming operation. By prioritizing responsible water management practices, fish farmers contribute to preserving the surrounding ecosystems, minimizing environmental impact, and ensuring the long-term viability of aquaculture.

To sum up, managing a fish farm well involves daily care, keeping an eye on growth, and ensuring a healthy environment. These practices not only benefit the fish but also contribute to a sustainable and successful fish farming operation.

Chapter 10:
Marketing and Selling Your Fishery Products

Now that you have successfully raised and cared for your fishes, it's time to focus on marketing and selling your products Effective marketing and selling of your fish products are pivotal components in the success of your fish farm. A well-structured marketing strategy not only increases brand visibility but also establishes a strong connection with your target audience. This guide delves into the realm of fishery product marketing and outlines strategies to enhance your reach, engage customers, and optimize profitability.

Understanding Your Market

Understanding who your customers are is crucial. It's about getting into their heads – knowing what they like, what they need, and how they buy things. Are you selling to locals who love fresh fish, fancy restaurants, bustling seafood markets, or big distributors who need loads of fish regularly?

Each type of customer has different wants and ways of doing things. The locals might care a lot about freshness and where their food comes from. Restaurants might want top-quality fish all the time. Seafood markets might want a variety of fish sizes and types. The big distributors might care most about getting a steady supply.

Knowing all this helps you make your fish and how you sell them just right for each type of customer. For example, you might talk about how you farm sustainably for the eco-conscious customers. Or maybe you highlight how versatile and top-notch your fish are for the fancy restaurants. Understanding what each customer group wants helps you tweak your fish and how you talk about them, making sure they hit the spot for each kind of buyer. This tailored approach makes it more likely your fish will be a hit with the folks you're trying to sell them to.

Marketing Strategies

Making an impact in the fish farming domain requires a mix of old-school and modern marketing approaches. To captivate different segments of your audience and establish a strong presence, you need a diverse marketing strategy.

Traditional Marketing Tactics

When it comes to promoting your fish farming business, don't discount the power of old-school techniques. Print ads, billboards, and active participation in local markets still pack a punch in grabbing attention. There's something about a well-placed ad in the local paper or a strategically positioned sign that catches the eye of people in the neighborhood.

Print Advertisements: Placing advertisements in local newspapers or magazines can be a game-changer. These ads tend to resonate with people who still love flipping through pages to catch up on local news. They're often more receptive to ads in publications they trust.

Strategic Signage: Utilizing signs strategically in high-traffic areas or near your farm can create local buzz. A cleverly designed sign can be the trigger that makes people stop and take notice, prompting them to inquire about your fish offerings.

Community Engagement: Being part of community events or trade shows provides invaluable face-to-face interaction. These events offer a chance to establish a personal connection with potential customers. Engaging directly with people allows you to tell your story, answer questions, and showcase your fish, fostering trust and familiarity.

These traditional methods might not seem as flashy as their digital counterparts, but they hold a certain charm and effectiveness, especially within local communities. They offer a tangible and personal touch that can leave a lasting impression on potential customers, making them an integral part of your marketing arsenal for your fish farming venture.

Modern Digital Strategies

In today's digital era, online platforms are treasure troves for marketing your fish farming business. Social media channels like Facebook, Instagram, and Twitter offer expansive reach to diverse audiences. Regularly sharing captivating content, such as glimpses into your farm life, intriguing insights about various fish species, or informative videos showcasing sustainable farming practices, can captivate people's interest and curiosity.

Social Media Engagement: These platforms are hubs of activity where your presence can work wonders. Sharing engaging content frequently helps build an interactive community around your farm. From behind-the-scenes shots of daily farm operations to intriguing trivia about different fish varieties, these snippets draw people in and make your farm more relatable.

The Power of a Website: Having a user-friendly website is paramount in the digital landscape. It serves as your online storefront, offering essential information about your farm, product range, and core values. It's the place where you narrate your story, exhibit customer testimonials, and provide a seamless platform for purchasing your fish online.

Virtual Showcase: Your website acts as a virtual showcase. It's not just about selling fish; it's about storytelling. You can detail your journey, illustrate your commitment to sustainability, and offer a deeper insight into your farming practices. Providing easy access to information and a smooth online shopping experience enhances customer satisfaction and trust.

By leveraging the potential of social media and a well-crafted website, you create a robust online presence for your fish farming venture. These platforms serve as bridges that connect you with a wider audience, enabling you to engage, inform, and entice potential customers, ultimately driving growth and success for your fish farming business.

The Influence of Informative Storytelling

Educating people about your products and the journey behind them is a potent tool. Sharing your farm's story, focusing on sustainability efforts, and highlighting the quality and freshness of your fish helps build a connection with customers. Giving insights into different fish species, their nutritional benefits, and eco-friendly farming practices can keep your audience engaged and informed.

A mix of old-school and new-age marketing is the way to go for fish farming success. Balancing traditional methods for local impact with digital strategies for broader outreach is crucial. Crafting compelling content, sharing your farm's narrative, and educating customers not only grabs attention but also builds trust and loyalty. Mastering these varied marketing avenues creates a robust strategy that boosts awareness, engagement, and ultimately, sales for your fish farming business.

Finding Different Ways to Sell Your Fish

When it comes to selling your fish, it's smart to try different approaches. You can sell directly to folks in your neighborhood at farmer's markets or set up your own shop. This way, you get to chat with people and show off your fish up close, letting them see how fresh and tasty they are.

Working with restaurants and grocery stores is another cool option. Restaurants often want top-quality seafood, so if your fish are fresh and fantastic, they might be interested. Plus, supplying to grocery stores means more people get to try your fish.

Teaming up with wholesalers is a big deal too. These guys handle larger sales, distributing to lots of places like supermarkets or other retailers. It's a way to get your fish out to a bigger audience.

But you know what's really key in all this? Building relationships with these buyers. Understanding what they need, being reliable with deliveries, and always having top-notch fish make a huge difference. It's about keeping these partnerships solid by being there for them and making sure they're happy with your fish.

By trying out different ways to sell and making sure your fish are top-notch, you'll build a network of buyers and keep your fish farming business running smoothly.

Ensure compliance with local and national regulations regarding fish farming, processing, and sales. Obtaining certifications for quality, sustainability, or organic practices can enhance your products' marketability and build trust with consumers. Stay adaptable and open to innovation in your marketing and sales approaches. Keep abreast of market trends, consumer preferences, and new technologies that can enhance your sales strategies and product offerings. Successfully marketing and selling your fish products requires a combination of market research, branding, effective sales channels, quality assurance, and customer engagement. By implementing strategic approaches tailored to your audience, you can establish a strong presence in the market and build a loyal customer base for your fish farming business.

Chapter 11:
Legal and Regulatory Requirements

Fishery farming, like any agricultural enterprise, is subject to a complex web of legal and regulatory requirements. Adhering to these regulations is not only a legal obligation but also a crucial step in ensuring the safety of your products, the welfare of your shoal, and the sustainability of your business. This guide delves into the realm of legal and regulatory requirements in fishery farming, providing insights into key areas that demand your attention.

Zoning and Land Use Regulations:

Before establishing your fishery farm, investigate local zoning laws to determine whether agricultural activities are permitted on your chosen land. Zoning regulations vary by location and may dictate the type and scale of fishery farming allowed. Obtaining the necessary permits and adhering to zoning requirements is fundamental to starting on the right legal footing.

Animal Welfare Standards:

Animal welfare regulations govern the treatment, care, and conditions of fishery on your farm. Compliance with these standards ensures that your fishes are raised in humane and ethical conditions. Regulations may cover aspects such as housing space, ventilation, access to clean water, and protection from extreme weather.

Food Safety and Inspection:

Fishery products are subject to rigorous food safety standards to protect consumers. Ensure that your farm follows recommended hygiene practices and adheres to regulations governing cleanliness, handling, processing, and storage of fishery products. Regular inspections and certifications may be required to demonstrate compliance.

Environmental Regulations:

Fishery farming has environmental implications, including waste management and potential impact on air and water quality. Familiarize yourself with regulations concerning waste disposal, nutrient management, and pollution control. Implement practices that minimize your farm's ecological footprint and align with sustainability goals.

Biosecurity Measures:

Biosecurity is crucial to preventing disease outbreaks. Many regions have regulations governing disease prevention and control measures on fishery farms. Implement biosecurity protocols, such as restricted access, disinfection, and proper waste disposal, to mitigate disease risks and comply with regulatory requirements.

Antibiotic and Medication Use:

Regulations surrounding antibiotic use in fishery farming are evolving. In many jurisdictions, antibiotics can only be used under veterinary supervision and in accordance with prescribed protocols. Understand local regulations on medication use, and work closely with a veterinarian to ensure responsible antibiotic administration.

Employment and Labor Laws:

If you employ staff on your fishery farm, you must adhere to labor laws that govern issues such as wages, working hours, safety standards, and worker rights. Complying with these laws creates a fair and legally sound work environment.

Labeling and Marketing Regulations:

Fishery product labeling and marketing are subject to specific regulations to ensure accurate and transparent information for consumers. Labels must include product information, nutritional content, allergen warnings, and other required details. Adhering to labeling standards builds consumer trust and avoids legal issues.

Traceability and Record Keeping:
Maintain detailed records of your fishery farm's operations, including feed purchases, veterinary treatments, shoal movements, and disease control measures. These records are crucial for traceability, compliance audits, and demonstrating adherence to regulations.

Export Requirements (If Applicable):
If you plan to export your fishery products, familiarize yourself with the export requirements of your target markets. These requirements may include specific health certifications, labeling standards, and documentation.

Running a fishery farm requires compliance with various legal and regulatory requirements. These requirements may include zoning regulations, environmental regulations, animal welfare regulations, food safety regulations, and employment regulations. By ensuring compliance with these regulations, you can operate your fishery farm legally and responsibly. In the next chapter, we'll explore the importance of record-keeping and data analysis for a successful fishery farm.

Chapter 12:
Record-Keeping and Data Analysis

Keeping accurate records and analyzing data is essential for the success of any business, including a fishery farm. The intricate task of maintaining comprehensive records and subjecting them to systematic analysis holds a transformative potential that can redefine the way fishery farms are managed. This comprehensive approach empowers fishery farmers to not only stay attuned to the ever-shifting nuances of their operations but also to wield data-driven insights to make strategic decisions that reverberate across all facets of their endeavors.

Record keeping serves as the bedrock upon which the edifice of efficient fishery management is constructed. The meticulous documentation of shoal health, feed consumption, medication administration, production rates, financial transactions, and more encapsulates the breadth of fishery farming intricacies. These records serve as a time capsule, enabling farmers to delve into historical data and unravel trends, patterns, and anomalies that might otherwise elude the naked eye. By crafting a narrative of your farm's journey through these records, you create an invaluable resource that underpins your decision-making process.

The repertoire of records to be maintained spans an extensive gamut, reflecting the multifaceted nature of fishery farming. From shoal inventory records that provide insight into the size and composition of your shoal, to the daily logs chronicling feed and water consumption that are integral to nutritional management, and the meticulous records of vaccinations and medication administration that safeguard shoal health – each piece contributes to the larger puzzle. Furthermore, records capturing egg production rates, mortality figures, and financial data enable a panoramic view of your farm's performance, steering your approach towards informed strategies and course corrections.

While traditional paper-based record keeping retains its value, the digital age offers sophisticated avenues for more efficient data management. Transitioning to digital databases or specialized fishery management software elevates record keeping to a realm of streamlined accuracy and accessibility. This shift not only reduces the risk of human error but also facilitates the extraction of insights through data analysis tools. These tools function as the conduit through which raw data is distilled into meaningful trends, correlations, and predictive insights that bear the potential to revolutionize your farm's trajectory.

Central to this process is the unwavering pursuit of consistency and accuracy. The designated individuals entrusted with the responsibility of record keeping play a pivotal role in upholding these standards. Regular training and oversight are essential to ensure data entry adheres to established protocols, preventing errors that could compromise the integrity of subsequent analysis. Because, in the world of data analysis, precision begets power. An erroneous entry can lead to skewed interpretations, which in turn can adversely impact your decision-making processes.

Data analysis doesn't merely involve the mechanistic examination of numbers; it's an art that uncovers hidden narratives within the data tapestry. By identifying key performance indicators (KPIs) tailored to your farm's objectives, you establish signposts that gauge the effectiveness of your strategies. Metrics like feed conversion ratio, mortality rate, egg production per hen, and overall shoal health serve as waypoints, guiding your assessment of progress and areas for refinement. Furthermore, benchmarking your farm against industry standards or peers elevates data analysis to a realm of perspective, shedding light on where you stand in the larger landscape.

The culmination of this data-driven journey is a cascade of informed decision-making. Armed with insights extracted from meticulously maintained records and astute analysis, you're empowered to steer your farm towards a trajectory of higher efficiency, improved productivity, and optimal resource allocation. Whether it's adjusting feed formulations to align with consumption trends, fine-tuning vaccination schedules to bolster shoal immunity, or anticipating potential health risks based on historical patterns, data-driven decisions transcend intuition to usher in an era of strategic precision.

In fact, data analysis even extends its reach into the realm of predictive modeling. By extrapolating trends from historical data, it lays the foundation for anticipating future outcomes. This proficiency proves invaluable in designing proactive disease prevention strategies, optimizing production schedules, and allocating resources with precision. It's a powerful tool that grants you a glimpse into the future, offering a strategic advantage in an industry where foresight can mean the difference between success and stagnation.

Yet, the journey doesn't culminate with a single cycle of data analysis. The beauty lies in its iterative nature. Regularly revisiting your records, analyzing emerging trends, and adapting your strategies based on empirical insights perpetuates a cycle of continuous learning and evolution. With each cycle, your knowledge deepens, your operations become more finely tuned, and your farm's potential for success grows exponentially.

In essence, record keeping and data analysis stand as the cornerstone of modern fishery farming. They provide the means to decode the intricacies of your operations, unravel the story your farm is telling through its data, and empower you to script a narrative of informed decisions and strategic precision. By establishing a robust system of record keeping, embracing digital tools, and unlocking the potential of data analysis, you not only optimize your farm's productivity and efficiency but also secure your position at the vanguard of the ever-evolving fishery farming landscape.

Chapter 13:
Scaling Your Fishery Business

Scaling a fish farm business involves strategic planning, resource management, and effective execution to expand operations while maintaining quality and sustainability.. Scaling your fishery farm demands a strategic blueprint that embraces growth while ensuring sustainability, efficiency, and animal welfare. This guide delves into the art of scaling fishery farms, incorporating insights into both the process of expansion and the crucial task of determining when the opportune moment for growth has arrived.

Market Research and Demand Assessment

Before you start ramping up your fish farm, it's crucial to dive into some serious market research. Think of it as your roadmap for the big expansion. This research helps you understand what people want, what's missing in the market, and how you can shape your growth plans to fit right in.

Checking Out Demand Trends: Keeping an eye on how much fish people want and when they want it is pretty important. You'll spot patterns in demand that can help you figure out which fish species to focus on when you're expanding.

Getting to Know What People Like: Understanding what buyers prefer when it comes to fish is key. Whether it's the type of fish, its size, how fresh it is, or how it's farmed, knowing these details helps you tweak your plans to meet what people are looking for.

Taking Stock of What's in Demand: It's not just about how much people want; it's also about what they want. Checking out what's hot in the market – be it certain fish species or particular types – helps you know where to aim when you're scaling up.

Sizing Up the Competition: Getting a good look at what your competitors are up to is smart. Studying what they're selling, how they're selling it, and how they're positioning themselves in the market helps you find your own unique spot. This helps you stand out and find your own way in the market.

By digging into the demand trends, customer likes, market needs, and what your competitors are doing, you'll get a solid grasp on what's needed in the market. This info becomes the building blocks for your expansion plans, making sure you're moving in sync with what the market wants.

Financial Planning

Expanding your fish farm is a big step that needs careful financial planning. To do it right, you've got to figure out how much it's going to cost. That means tallying up everything from building new stuff like ponds or tanks, getting fancier tech, hiring more people, and covering the extra day-to-day costs.

Once you've got a grip on the numbers, it's time to think about where the money's coming from. You might need to get a loan from a bank, find investors who believe in your plan and want to invest, or use your own profits to finance the expansion. Making sure you've got the right financial backing is key to making your expansion plans a reality without breaking the bank.

Infrastructure and Facilities Expansion

When you're thinking about growing your fish farm, it's not just about dreaming big; it's about making real changes on the ground. Expanding means beefing up or even creating new stuff to make your farm bigger and better. This could mean putting up more ponds, adding extra tanks, or setting up new cages. Or maybe it's about getting cool new tech that helps you produce more fish. But here's the catch: whatever you add or upgrade needs to match what your farm really needs, and most importantly, it needs to keep up the quality.

Building More Infrastructure: Expanding means getting your hands dirty, maybe quite literally. You might need to dig more ponds, set up bigger tanks, or install new cages. Making these additions should fit in perfectly with what your farm requires, like if you're aiming for specific fish species or trying to increase production.

Investing in Advanced Technology: Getting the latest and greatest tech can be a game-changer. Upgrading to tech that helps you produce more fish efficiently can boost your farm's capacity. But remember, it's not just about having fancy gadgets; it's about how well they fit in with your farm's goals and quality standards.

Ensuring that any expansion or upgrade aligns perfectly with your farm's specific needs and maintains the high quality you're known for is crucial. It's not just about growing bigger; it's about growing smarter, making changes that truly make your fish farm even better than before.

Scaling your fish farm business requires careful planning, investment, and adaptation to market demands while ensuring sustainable and high-quality practices. By addressing these key aspects, you can navigate the scaling process effectively and position your business for long-term success and growth in the competitive fish farming industry.

Conclusion

Congratulations on completing this guide to starting a fishery farm! In the world of fish farming, success hinges on a delicate balance of innovation, dedication, and adaptability. As we close this book, it's clear that fish farming isn't just about rearing fish; it's a symphony of science, sustainability, and market savvy.

From the humble beginnings of aquaculture to the intricacies of selecting the right fish species, designing farm structures, managing water quality, and understanding market dynamics, the journey of fish farming is multifaceted. We've explored the depths of feeding strategies, health management, and the critical role of consumer behavior in shaping the industry.

Scaling a fish farm is no small feat, and it demands strategic foresight, financial prudence, and a deep understanding of market trends. It's about not just expanding but doing so responsibly, ensuring that growth aligns with sustainability principles and maintains the highest quality standards.

Throughout this journey, one theme has remained constant: the resilience and adaptability of the fish farming community. Whether adapting to environmental changes, market shifts, or technological advancements, fish farmers have displayed a remarkable ability to evolve and thrive in an ever-changing landscape.

As we conclude this book, let's carry forward the essence of sustainable fish farming, where innovation meets responsibility, and where the future is shaped by a commitment to nourishing both people and the planet. The story of fish farming is ever-evolving, and it's our collective responsibility to ensure it continues to flourish for generations to come.

www.ingramcontent.com/pod-product-compliance
Lightning Source LLC
Chambersburg PA
CBHW062249290526
45794CB00006B/2477